SECRETS EXPOSED
What Men Know About Women
(Unabridged Edition)

INCLUDES SECRET ADDENDUM:
Husbandry 101

by R. Scott Alvord

Secrets Exposed – What Men Know About Women (Unabridged Edition) ™
Includes Secret Addendum: **Husbandry 101**
By:
R. Scott Alvord, MBA-MCA, BSCS

(NOTE: Both of the above degrees are technical degrees…nerd degrees…logical degrees…right?)

★ Copyright © 2023-2024, R. Scott Alvord and Advanced Publishing Concepts. All Rights Reserved ★

No part of this publication may be reproduced, stored in a retrieval system, or transmitted in any form or by any means, electronic, mechanical, photocopying, recording, scanning, or otherwise, without the prior written permission of the author and the publishing company.

Limit of Liability/Disclaimer of Warranty: While the publisher and author have used their best efforts in preparing this book, they make no representations or warranties with respect to the accuracy or completeness of the contents of this book, and specifically disclaim any implied warranties of merchantability or fitness for a particular purpose. No warranty may be created or extended by sales representatives or written sales materials. The comments, advice, and strategies contained herein may not be suitable for your situation. You should consult with a professional when appropriate. The publisher, author, and editing team shall not be liable for any loss of profit or any other damages, including but not limited to special, incidental, consequential, personal, or other damages.   …this includes marital or relationship problems! **This book was written for entertainment purposes and if you try to use it as a marriage or relationship guide…well…it's kinda like Darwin's Survival of the Fittest, you risk becoming extinct!**

1. Humor: Men, Women & Relationships 2. Humor: Marriage & Family
3. Humor: General 4. Wit and Humor
ISBN: 978-1-942836-69-8   (v1.2)

Cover design & book design by Advanced Publishing Concepts
The text of this book is set in Cambria font. Printed in the United States of America

Advanced Publishing Concepts
(a division of Advanced Development Concepts, LLC)
141 Bogart Ct., Roseville, CA 95747 | (916) 782-4272
www.AdvancedPublishingConcepts.com
www.WhatMenKnowAboutWomen.com

Secrets Exposed – What Men Know About Women (Unabridged Edition) ™

Includes Secret Addendum: **Husbandry 101**

By:

R. Scott Alvord

IMPORTANT: If you appreciate the humor in this book and would like to give back or thank the author, PLEASE leave a review at Amazon and/or other major book resellers as positive reviews boost rankings. If you didn't enjoy this book…well…ummm…hey, no need to waste your time. ☺

Copyright © 2023-2024, Advanced Publishing Concepts (All rights reserved)

This page was intentionally left blank.

Dedication & Acknowledgments

Most people skip dedication sections in books, but I do encourage you to at least read the "And finally…" section at the bottom of this dedication.

This book is dedicated to the wonderful women in my life:

My beautiful and intelligent bride, Karen: Thank you for taking me on as a project. I love the 4 years we dated through college and the 37+ years as a married couple. You make life fun and mysterious, and you certainly ensure that I never think that I'm perfect. I love you for making me a better person every day…or at least, maybe every few days.

My dear mother, Sharon: You not only gave birth to me, but you taught me about Christ, and ethics, and how to respect and appreciate the women in my life. Thank you, Mom. I grew up in an era when women did most of the housework and while I thought it seemed normal at the time, I look back and it pains me to see how hard you worked for our family. Thank you. In the Addendum section of this book, I play on those 70's and 80's stereotypes to allow men to "strategically" have the "freedom" that you allowed Dad. I do it for comedy purposes only and I want to assure you that I'm not taking modern marriages trivially since they should indeed require equal effort in the home.

My two sisters, Vandy and Corinne: You both taught our brother Brett and I that girls are very different from boys. We had a blast as kids. Brett and I enjoyed you both as sisters. But I still maintain that it was not fair that you could get away with anything just by batting your eyelashes and acting innocent. We all know the truth. (grin)

My four wonderful daughters, Nikki, Chrissi, Dawn, and Sharna: Wow, what an exciting experience trying to raise you along with your three brothers. All unique, all different, yet the four of you and your mother could read each other's mind and us dudes didn't have a chance at getting the upper hand in anything.

My two daughters-in-law, Brianna and Ashlynn: Thank you for loving our sons and helping them see the intricacies of partnering with wonderful women to make their lives so much better as husbands and parents.

My granddaughters, Maddison, Zaria, Izzy, Reagan, Peyton, and Chelsea. I'm so proud of you. You're often the center of attention and while I think you have wonderful personalities and are much easier to raise than your parents were, I kinda secretly hope you give your parents a little payback so when you're all grown up and on your own, they can look back with a big smile like I do.

To the women (mostly nurses) I worked with at the AH corporate office, thank you for helping me grow up professionally and learn that the way "logical" male programmers think is incredibly different (like from a galaxy far, far away) than compassionate female nurses. I gained respect and appreciation for looking at things differently.

To the many ladies that worked for me at our restaurant, A Dash of Panache: Thank you for making our work environment fun and giving great service to our variety of guests. You taught me a lot about listening first before I assume what is being said and realizing that what I say can hurt feelings if I don't take the time to choose my words more carefully.

To Maggie and Ellie (our Dorkie and Chiweenie pups): Thank you for being my psychotic buddies who offer unconditional love that I certainly need at times.

I also want to sincerely thank the many people who worked on various informal teams as we researched these topics and discussed how to present them. Both men and women alike contributed equally, and it all came together like magic. My friends on social media were excellent topic resources too! The draft advisory team, who helped edit or contribute to portions of this book without taking overall (or any) responsibility for it, included: Kelly Kozub, Mike Sarantakos, Anthony Smits, Dan Beal, Keith Egelston, Alyson Smith, John Javidan, Scott Milligan, Karen Alvord, Camilo Arellano Jr., and others who wanted to remain anonymous.

And finally, to those of you with a great sense of humor who love and appreciate the differences between men and women: I sincerely hope you enjoy this book. I whole-heartedly admit that us guys are the weaker gender and I hope the humor you find in this book celebrates that weakness!

I do want to be CLEAR that this book is written for entertainment purposes <u>only</u> and if you are offended…well…re-read this sentence. Also, if you choose to really follow the "secret" techniques detailed in the Addendum, you might find yourself sleeping on a couch until you wake back up into the reality of modern marriages.

Sincerely,

Scott

This page was intentionally left blank.

Foreword by Karen Alvord (The Author's Wife)

Yes, I'm the better half and Scott knows it. At the time of the publication of this book, he and I will have been married for over 37 years. Together, we have raised seven children into adulthood, and we now enjoy thirteen grandchildren. Our home has always been full of laughter, in large part to Scott's unique sense of humor.

When Scott told me what his next book would be about, I laughed. Why? Because I KNOW how much he "knows" about the way women think. I was pretty sure he wouldn't have enough material for a social media post, much less a book.

However, I can attest that my husband put a LOT of diligent research into this book. He met with men's groups, marriage counselors, business groups, and even strangers on the street. He talked with couples that have been married more than fifty years, just to gain insight into the comprehensive revelations he gathered for your enjoyment. He even travelled the globe…well he surfed his social media connections far and wide to test his assumptions, striving for accurate content.

Although Scott refused to allow me to read the Addendum section, claiming it was "for men only," I did read absolutely everything else in this book. I CAN OFFICIALLY ATTEST THAT SCOTT ALVORD WAS 100% ACCURATE IN HIS THOROUGH EXPLANATION OF WHAT MEN TRULY KNOW ABOUT WOMEN.

I want to add that there may be a few women who don't appreciate the content of this book. I encourage these sisters in humanity to lighten up a bit and realize that we are indeed unique creatures, and our complexities are far beyond the complete comprehension of our male counterparts. We women are to be celebrated! That includes our ability to multitask, love chocolate, create new life within us, and many other stereotypical characteristics that Scott has touched on in this book. While Scott certainly isn't a perfect husband, he has been a strong partner and does a lot more than he gives himself credit for in this book. (Though don't get me started about his cooking and laundry skills!) I do appreciate Scott's humor, even if it is sometimes eye-rolling worthy.

And to my secret sisters playing "the scoring game," I want you to know that I still frequently get the top score in my region. (wink, wink!)

Karen Alvord, MBA, LCSW

Secrets Exposed – What Men Know About Women (Unabridged Edition) ™

Table of Contents

"The only reason I'd ever get a sex change operation is to see what it's like to be right all the time." – Brian Wilson

Page	Chapter/Section
5	Dedication & Acknowledgments
9	Foreword by Karen Alvord (The Author's Wife)
11	Table of Contents
15	Historical Understanding of Women (Prehistoric to Modern)
47	Insider Knowledge to Decipher Her Emotions
69	Foolproof Techniques for Successfully Arguing with Women
91	The Discovered Reasons Why Women Go to the Bathroom in Groups
115	Mysteries of Women's Handbags Exposed
139	Navigating the Double-Edged Sword of Complimenting Women Without Being Misunderstood
153	Foolproof Answers for the Dangerous *"Does This Make Me Look Fat?"* Question
155	Comprehensive Insights into Why Women's Shopping Habits Require So Much Time Compared to Men's
179	Secrets Behind Why Women Are So Great at Multitasking
203	How to Guarantee Your Beautiful Woman Feels Beautiful

219	Proven Techniques to Ensure She Will Be on Time
241	Why Women are More Talkative Than Men
265	Men's Insights into the Real Reason for All Those Pillows
281	How Women can Tell the Color Difference between Off-White, Ivory, Vanilla, Cream, Ecru, Eggshell, Beige, Linen, Buff, and Dove
305	Unmistakably Understanding What Intimacy Means to Her
321	How to Guarantee the Intimacy You Desire
343	Techniques for Handling Menstrual Cycles Like a Pro
359	Pregnancy: Proven Knowledge for Dealing with All Nine Months
375	Everything the Best Dads Know About Their Daughters (Birth to Empty Nest)
387	Tips for Understanding What Her Girlfriends Are Saying About You
403	Her Magical Intuition and How to Avoid Becoming Its Victim
417	If Divorce Happens, How to Avoid Getting Taken to the Cleaners
427	What Artificial Intelligence Understands About Women
435	Hints & Signals: Translate the Code and Read Between the Lines
443	The Supernatural Connection Between Women and Chocolate
449	Conclusive Research Explaining the Enigma of "Nothing's Wrong" When Clearly Something Is
455	All Other Information That Men Know About Women

467	**Addendum: Husbandry 101** – Secrets Only Men Know. Selected Excerpts
467	• **Gentlemen, DO NOT SHARE THIS WITH WOMEN or you'll be required to turn in your Man Card!**
469	• **Lifetime Liberation from Laundry**
469	• Classic Bait and Switch
470	• Crayola Explosion
471	• Drying With Purpose
472	• Folding Clothes to Keep Wrinkles In
473	• Wash, Rinse, Repeat
473	• Disclaimer
475	• **Cooking for Freedom**
475	• Prepare the Groundwork
478	• Manstakes for the Most Memorable Meal
478	• Setting the Table
479	• It Takes Meat Balls
480	• The Limp Spaghetti Conundrum
480	• Sassy Sauce
481	• Crunchy Salad
481	• Bring Home the Bread
482	• Having Your Cake and Not Eating It Too

482	• The Closing Act
484	• Avoid Getting Sucked Back into the Kitchen
485	• Reward Her for Your Freedom
487	**• Maintaining BBQ Grill Master Status**
487	• The Setup
488	• Gaslighting
489	• Get Her Cooking
489	• The Final Lap
490	• The Barb was Queued Up
493	**• The Secret Point System Game That Women Play**
493	• The Deets
494	• The Score is Against You
494	• Marbled Sunscreen
495	• Phone Call at Work
495	• Hold Her Purse
496	• Wearing Girlyman Clothes
497	• Shopping Cart Humiliation
498	• Run to the Store for "A Few Things"
499	• Rolling with the Punches

Historical Understanding of Women (Prehistoric to Modern)

"Until Eve arrived, this was a man's world." – Richard Armour

"Women and cats will do as they please, and men and dogs should relax and get used to the idea." – Robert A. Heinlein

Below is a detailed historical understanding of women passed down through the ages from way back when women gathered berries for men and swept animal bones out of caves:

This page was intentionally left blank.

Insider Knowledge to Decipher Her Emotions

"Women aren't confusing. They're a Sudoku-Jenga-puzzle surrounded by Rubix cubes strapped to [someone] screaming at you in another language." – Mike Vanatta

"Men also have feelings. For example, they can feel hungry." – Seen on a T-shirt

"Deciphering a woman's emotions is like trying to read a book in a language you don't speak, blindfolded, and with the book closed." – [Name withheld by request]

Like spaghetti, her emotions are often tangled up so you're never quite sure where one feeling ends and another begins. From tears to silence, below is *everything* that men have gathered as insider knowledge about women that helps decipher her emotional clues:

This page was intentionally left blank.

Foolproof Techniques for Successfully Arguing with Women

"There are two theories to arguing with a woman. Neither works." – Will Rogers

"Some women (and here I'm referring to my wife) can share as many as three days' worth of feelings about an event that took eight seconds to actually happen." – Dave Barry

"A woman has the last word in any argument. Anything a man says after that is the beginning of another argument." – Anonymous

"The secret to winning an argument with a woman: They have to be dead." – John Betz, Jr.

Unless one of you is comatose, there will definitely be disagreements and sometimes arguments. As men, we are naturally competitive and we certainly don't want to lose an argument, especially when we're defending a valid position. Below is *every* foolproof technique known to man that can be used to successfully win an argument with a woman:

This page was intentionally left blank.

The Discovered Reasons Why Women Go to the Bathroom in Groups

"Men go it alone to take a break from friends, family, and social events. Women go in groups to take a break from men." – Camilo Arellano, Jr.

"Women go together so they have someone to hold and protect their purse. Men leave someone at the table to watch and protect their beer." – Scott Milligan

"Women go for the plot; men go for the plop." – John Javidan

Surprise! It is NOT because they need someone to watch the door while they do their business in private! Below is *everything* that experts have gathered as factual insider knowledge about *why* women go to the bathroom in groups:

This page was intentionally left blank.

Mysteries of Women's Handbags Exposed

"You don't touch the purse. The purse is sacrosanct." – Julie James

"A woman's mind is as complex as the contents of her handbag; even when you get to the bottom of it, there is ALWAYS something at the bottom to surprise you!" – Billy Connolly

"I always carry multipurpose products in my handbag." – Ashley Madekwe

Once you know the secrets of these expensive, portable mystery purses and what's inside them, you'll be far ahead of most men. Below is *everything* that experts have exposed about the mysteries of women's handbags (purses):

This page was intentionally left blank.

Navigating the Double-Edged Sword of Complimenting Women Without Being Misunderstood

"Trying to understand a woman's mind is like trying to solve a Rubik's Cube blindfolded – just when you think you've got it, everything changes!" – Anonymous (wisely by choice)

"Women have more imagination than men. They need it to tell us how wonderful we are." – Arnold H. Glasow

"There are only three things women need in life: food, water, and compliments." – Chris Rock

All men can empathize that being misunderstood in this situation is generally unavoidable, just like taxes. Below is *all* knowledge that men have accumulated regarding how to safely navigate the process of complimenting women without being misunderstood:

This page was intentionally left blank.

Foolproof Answers for the Dangerous *"Does this Make Me Look Fat?"* Question

"The 'Does this make me look fat?' question is like a pop quiz from high school – no matter how you answer, you're gonna fail!" – [Name withheld by request]

"The most terrifying thing any woman can say to me is 'Notice anything different?'" – Mike Vanatta

Also known as the "Question from hell." After extensive research and trial testing, the following is a complete list of *all* the foolproof answers to that extremely dangerous and tricky question:

This page was intentionally left blank.

Comprehensive Insights into Why Women's Shopping Habits Require So Much Time Compared to Men's

"The odds of going to the store for a loaf of bread and coming out with only a loaf of bread are three billion to one." – Erma Bombeck

"Women's shopping is like a scenic route through a beautiful landscape, complete with detours, sightseeing, and spontaneous picnics. Men's shopping is more like a race to the finish line with the fewest pit stops." – [Name withheld by request]

"I've been shopping all my life and still have nothing to wear." – Sally Poplin

"Shopping is better than sex. If you're not satisfied after shopping, you can exchange it for something you really like." – Adrienne Gusoff

Us men be like: "*I need something, so I go to the closest store and buy it.*" But our female counterparts don't relate to that logic in the slightest. After extensive research, below is *everything* that men know about why women's shopping habits require so much time:

This page was intentionally left blank.

Secrets Behind Why Women Are So Great at Multitasking

"If women are so bloody perfect at multitasking, how come they can't have a headache and sex at the same time?" – Billy Connolly

"Whatever women do they must do twice as well as men to be thought half as good. Luckily this is not difficult." – Charlotte Whitton

Parallel processing in computers is essential for getting things done quickly, but how in the world can our ladies seem to accomplish so much in so little time? Below is *everything* men have compiled as insights into *why* women are so great at multitasking:

This page was intentionally left blank.

How to Guarantee Your Beautiful Woman Feels Beautiful

"To judge from the covers of countless women's magazines, the two topics most interesting to women are (1) Why men are all disgusting pigs, and (2) How to attract men." – Dave Barry

"Scientists now believe that the primary biological function of breasts is to make men stupid." – Dave Barry

How you say it without sounding insincere, aloof, or creepy means all the difference in the world and in your relationship. After decades of intense research and testing, below is *everything* that men have figured out regarding how to ensure that the important woman in your life feels beautiful:

This page was intentionally left blank.

Proven Techniques to Ensure She Will Be on Time

"When my wife says she'll be ready in 5 minutes, I know I have just enough time to fly to space and write a poem on the moon before we go."
– Mike Vanatta

"The world is my runway, and I arrive fashionably late to my own show."
– Seen on a T-shirt

"I am invariably late for appointments — sometimes as much as two hours. I've tried to change my ways but the things that make me late are too strong, and too pleasing." – Marilyn Monroe

She's on time for things that are important to her, so why the heck is she making your life miserable about arriving on time for what's important to you? Below is *every* proven technique that the most experienced men know to ensure she will be on time:

This page was intentionally left blank.

Why Women are More Talkative Than Men

"She speaks ten words a second - with gusts to fifty." – Southern Saying

"The measure of a man is his silence. The measure of a woman is her elocution. Beware of an overly talkative man and an inordinately silent woman." – Abhaidev (The Influencer: Speed Must Have a Limit)

"If Miss Elton spoke water instead of words, then there would have been a repetition of Noah's flood." – Kellyn Roth (The Dressmaker's Secret)

It takes her an hour to recap a five-minute encounter and not only have you used up your allotted words for the day, you also know you're gonna blow the pop quiz that she'll give you at the end of her story! Why is she so talkative? Below is the result of *everything* experts know about why women are more talkative than men:

This page was intentionally left blank.

Men's Insights into the Real Reason for All Those Pillows

"The pillow-to-woman ratio is directly proportional to the level of comfort and inversely proportional to available storage space!" – Every man

"You can never have too many pillows." – Every woman

"Behind every woman with a mountain of pillows is a man wondering why he is expected to restack them in the same pattern." – [Name withheld by request]

The pillow mountain seems to use a flexible and subjective formula for determining the right number of pillows for every situation. Too bad men have no clue what that formula looks like! Below is *everything* that men know about the real reasons for all those pillows:

This page was intentionally left blank.

How Women can Tell the Color Difference between Off-White, Ivory, Vanilla, Cream, Ecru, Eggshell, Beige, Linen, Buff, and Dove

"Women are a walking Ninja with a Pantone color guide while men are still stuck in a black and white movie!" – Chat GPT

"Women have a secret superpower: spotting the subtle shades of color that leave men utterly clueless!" – Seen on a T-shirt

"Emotions are the colors of the soul; they are spectacular and incredible. When you don't feel, the world becomes dull and colorless." – Wm. Paul Young

"Colors, like features, follow the changes of the emotions." – Pablo Picasso

It's more like Fifty Shades of Frustration as two colors held next to each other look the same to a man but have different names that all women recognize. Below is *everything* known to man that can scientifically explain how women can tell the subtle differences in colors:

This page was intentionally left blank.

Unmistakably Understanding What Intimacy Means to Her

"I miss crawling into a man's arm, kissing his neck, saying those three little words into his ear, 'And another thing...'" – Felicia Michaels

"You know that look women get when they want to have sex? Me neither." – Steve Martin

"Women are definitely more interested in muscles than a sense of humor. You will never hear a woman say, 'I wish Brad Pitt would put his shirt back on and tell some jokes.'" – Dave Barry

"I asked my wife, 'On a scale from one to ten, how do you rate me as a lover?' She said, 'You know I'm no good at fractions.'" – Rodney Dangerfield

Understand the subtle messaging and expectations once and for all! Below is *everything* that men know about how to unmistakably understand what intimacy means to her:

This page was intentionally left blank.

How to Guarantee the Intimacy You Desire

"My wife is a sex object – every time I ask for sex, she objects." – Les Dawson

"There are a number of mechanical devices which increase sexual arousal, particularly in women. Chief among these is the Mercedes-Benz 380SL convertible." – P. J. O'Rourke

"Women are like diesel engines. And what I mean by that is it may take a little while to get 'em warmed up, but once you do, they can run a long, long time. Whereas, men, on the other hand, men are more like bottle rockets." – Jeff Foxworthy

"Love is like a fart, if you force it, it's probably crap." – Joe Wiley

We're pretty sure you turned to this chapter first, right? You both want intimacy but somehow the expectations are rarely in sync, and it seems you're the one getting the short end of the deal. Below is *everything* compiled as insights into techniques to guarantee the type and frequency of the intimacy men desire:

This page was intentionally left blank.

Techniques for Handling Menstrual Cycles Like a Pro

"From what I understand about the female experience, the period should be called something more drastic, like the exclamation point." – Ruminations.com

"If women ran the world we wouldn't have wars, just intense negotiations every 28 days." – Robin Williams

"Periods help you learn how to get blood off things, which is probably why you hear more stories of men being caught for murder." – [Name withheld by request]

"If men had periods, menstrual leave would be a universally accepted thing, and companies would offer paid time off for 'feeling kind of murder-y today.'" – FSMStatistics.fm

Does she seem moody, miserable, and sometimes murderous? Mastering menstrual cycles is what legends are made of! Below is a compiled list of *all* known techniques for expertly handling menstrual cycles like a pro:

This page was intentionally left blank.

Pregnancy: Proven Knowledge for Dealing with All Nine Months

"Hormones and no alcohol. Interact at your own risk." – [Name withheld by request]

"She was discounted by Mattel because a pregnant doll was just too weird." – Narrator (Barbie)

"Danger, due to the influence of pregnancy hormones I could burst into tears or kill you in the next five minutes." – [Name withheld by request]

"Months have an average of 30 days, except the 9th month of pregnancy which has about 1,000 days." – Seen on a T-shirt

The start and end games are incredible, but the road between pregnancy and childbirth is akin to being a bewildered character in a thriller movie, where you're just trying to survive the plot twists, cravings, and scary moments! Below is *all* proven knowledge that experts have gathered to help men deal with all nine months of pregnancy:

This page was intentionally left blank.

Everything the Best Dads Know About Their Daughters (Birth to Empty Nest)

"My daughter got me a 'World's Best Dad' mug. So, we know she's sarcastic." – Bob Odenkirk

"A little girl giggles when she is denied an ice cream by her mother. She knows daddy will get her some later." – Anonymous

"My fingers may be small, but I've got my dad wrapped around them." – Seen on a teen's T-shirt

The daddy-daughter relationship can be like a sitcom where you are the lead character of the show and your daughter, and her friends, are the critics in the live audience. But knowledge is the key to being a star. Below is *everything* that the best dads truly know about their daughters, regardless of age:

This page was intentionally left blank.

Tips for Understanding What Her Girlfriends are Saying About You

"A woman without a man is like a fish without a bicycle." – Gloria Steinem

"If a man is talking in the forest, and no woman is there to hear him, is he still wrong?" – Seen on a mug, on the desk of a female executive

"Well, you know what they say: If you don't have anything nice to say about anybody, come sit by me." – Clairee Belcher (Steel Magnolias)

You know they are talking about you and the only way to prepare a proper defense is to understand their playbook. Below is *comprehensive* knowledge and tips for understanding what her friends are saying about you:

This page was intentionally left blank.

Her Magical Intuition and How to Avoid Becoming Its Victim

"Feminine intuition is a fiction and a fraud. It is nonsensical, illogical, emotional, ridiculous, and practically foolproof." – Harry Haenigsen

"My last girlfriend had a memory so good she could remember things that never happened." – Greg Tamblyn

"I would rather trust a woman's instinct than a man's reason." – Stanley Baldwin

Her intuition is amazing and incredible, but not when it's used against you. Below is *everything* that men know about a woman's intuition. This also contains comprehensive advice on how to avoid becoming a victim of that intuition:

This page was intentionally left blank.

If Divorce Happens, How to Avoid Getting Taken to the Cleaners

"A jealous woman does better research than the FBI." – Seen on a T-shirt

"Instead of getting married again, I'm going to find a woman I don't like and just give her a house." – Lewis Grizzard

"Marriages don't last. When I meet a guy, the first question I ask myself is: is this the man I want my children to spend their weekends with?" – Rita Rudner

"When I divorced, I went through the various stages of grieving: anger, denial, and dancing around with my settlement check." – Maura Kennedy

"In our family we don't divorce our men – we bury them." – Ruth Gordon

"To be fair, in most divorces the house is split evenly. The women get the inside, the men get the outside." – Bruce @BruceForce

Many men have been down this path that is laden with the shattered bones of those that failed before them. Below is *everything* that experts have accumulated to help men avoid getting taken to the cleaners in a divorce:

This page was intentionally left blank.

What Artificial Intelligence Understands About Women

"They say AI knows everything, but when it comes to understanding women, we're still deciphering the code." – Chat GPT

"AI can analyze complex data, but decoding the female mind is a challenge even for the smartest algorithms." – An embarrassed Mac Pro

A man's mere mortal intelligence pales in comparison to a woman's, thus forcing him to turn to computers to get answers. Below is *everything* that the advanced algorithms of artificial intelligence (AI) understand about women:

This page was intentionally left blank.

Hints & Signals: Translate the Code and Read Between the Lines

"A woman can say more in a sigh than a man can say in a sermon." – Arnold Haultain

"The problem with life is, by the time you can read women like a book, your library card has expired." – Milton Berle

You are pretty sure there is more to that response than she is showing on the surface; but your happiness during the next hour, day, or year will depend on how quickly you decipher the message in time to respond appropriately. Below is *everything* that men have figured out regarding women's unspoken language of hints and signals, and how to translate into words that a man can understand while reading between the lines of what she says:

This page was intentionally left blank.

The Supernatural Connection Between Women and Chocolate

"92 percent of self-described chocolate addicts are female." – Rory Evans (NBC News)

"Chocolate is really a problem. I'm trying to be healthy right now, so I'll eat carob chips, which are kind of like chocolate. But sometimes I'll have a midnight snack, and I'll wake up, and I'll find chocolate in my bed." – Claire Holt

"'Man cave' seems retrograde, but 'she shed' seems progressive. Or maybe it's just a place for me to eat embarrassing amounts of chocolate in private." – Faith Salie

"Chocolate: the one thing that's never let a woman down." – Anonymous

You can't buy her happiness, but you can buy her chocolate, and that's kind of the same thing. Below is *everything* that men have discovered through scientific research that explains the supernatural connection between women and chocolate:

This page was intentionally left blank.

Conclusive Research Explaining the Enigma of "Nothing's Wrong" When Clearly Something Is

"She claims he's the strong, silent type, but we all know he's just too scared to interrupt her!" – Seen on a T-shirt

"Want to stump an AI? Ask it to explain what women really mean when they say 'fine.'" – Chat GPT answering for itself

"When a woman says nothing's wrong, that means everything's wrong. And when a woman says everything's wrong, that means everything's wrong! And when a woman says something's not funny, you'd better not laugh your ass off!" – Homer

When men hear the statement, "Nothing is wrong," they know that a tornado is about to touch down while they are standing in the middle of a rickety old shed with sharp garden tools hanging on the walls. Below is *everything* that men know about how to understand and handle the "Nothing's wrong" statement:

This page was intentionally left blank.

All Other Information That Men Know About Women

"Despite my thirty years of research into the woman soul, I have not yet been able to answer the great question that has never been answered: What does a woman want?" - Sigmund Freud

"Barbie is all these women. And all these women are Barbie." - Narrator (Barbie)

"If this got out, this could mean extremely weird things for our world." - Will Ferrel (Barbie)

"What I don't understand is how women can pour hot wax on their bodies, let it dry, then rip out every single hair by its root and still be scared of spiders." - Jerry Seinfeld

"Blame Mattel. They made the rules." - Kate McKinnon (Weird Barbie)

All of the previous chapters cover a lot of known information on popular topics. This chapter is the catch-all for the other known information that doesn't fit neatly into other categories. Below is *ALL* other uncategorized information that men know about women:

This page was intentionally left blank.

Addendum: Husbandry 101 – Secrets Only Men Know

Selected Excerpts

Gentlemen, DO NOT SHARE THIS WITH WOMEN or you'll be required to turn in your Man Card!

"Not having your man card for so long has clearly turned your brain to mush." – Reese Monroe

Man Card (noun) – "Requirement to be accepted as a respectable member of the male community. Can and should be revoked by other respectable males for doing non-respectable-male things. Example: We had to take away Henry's Man Card because he cried in public when Kristina dumped him." – Urban Dictionary

"Turn in your man card" (phrase) – "Instructional phrase (spoken in a manner which can only be termed as pure disgust) used by one male to another male who has clearly shown he has lost all vestige of manhood." – Urban Dictionary

IMPORTANT! It is critically important to understand that THIS chapter is to never ever EVER be shared with women! Just like the zillions of secrets they have, us men need to maintain the top-secret status of these husbandry tips and tricks. IF YOU PLAN TO KEEP THIS BOOK ON DISPLAY IN PUBLIC, you MUST tear out this addendum, burn it, and then flush the ashes! Anyone

Copyright © 2023-2024, Advanced Publishing Concepts (All rights reserved)

failing to keep this material top secret will be required to turn in their Man Card and hold a purse near the checkout stands of Wal-Mart for a solid hour!

You've been warned.

NOTE: These are only excerpts, taken from the full Husbandry 101 manuscript. Yes, it's a manuscript, almost holy because of the wisdom and power, but not in any way sacrilegious. However, the full manuscript of Husbandry 101 is never shown together because if it ever got into the hands of women, our manly world would end as we know it. Manhood and freedom would be eliminated, and women would rule the world with ultimate power.

Lifetime Liberation from Laundry

"Marriage is about the most expensive way for the average man to get laundry done." – Burt Reynolds

"Alexa, do the laundry!" – [dreamed everyone who ever owned an Alexa]

"It will all come out in the wash." – Anonymous

This confidential chapter teaches husbands how to enjoy a lifetime of never being asked to do the laundry again. Of course, you are "willing" to do your share of the laundry, but after executing this playbook, you will be banned from the laundry like a mime from a karaoke party!

Classic Bait and Switch
In a nutshell, to be relieved from *ever* doing laundry again, you must ensure your spouse never *wants* you to do laundry again! Yes, a true win-win that only skilled husbands can pull off!

So, as early in the marriage as possible, you should lovingly volunteer to do the laundry and insist you do not need any help. In reality, you don't want help because you don't want a witness.

Timing is important though. You need the dirty clothes to contain things that will be...well...umm...memorable later. Pay attention to what goes in the dirty clothes pile. You want bright colors, delicates, things that normally need special attention when washed or dried. Oh yes, you absolutely will give them very special attention!

Crayola Explosion

It's all about a lasting reminder that you apparently suck at doing laundry. Getting colors to run and stain other clothing, especially white clothing, is what legacies are built on. Years down the road when your spouse tells this story, it needs to be epic for sure.

Don't worry about what your married buddies will think because they'll either be amazed at the depth of what you pulled off or they will realize they are just wusses and you're a real man. Either way, they'll know not to share that it was purposeful. Women will be aghast at the horror or they will completely relate because their own husband is horrible at laundry too. Regardless, it will indeed be legendary.

Let's pause here for a moment. What you read above and what you are about to read below will be legendary, yes, but it will ruin some clothes and it will hurt your relationship to a degree that you will need to work to repair. Before you continue with these proven techniques, sit back and think about the desire to be free from laundry vs the desire to cause stress in your relationship. (this text will pause while you make a decision...)

Well, you're still reading so this assumes you're willing to go for it. Hang on for a memorable ride!

The key is ensuring that the whites that go into the laundry are pink or a tie dye when they come out! Your wife will wash colors together in cold water and whites separately in warm water. You? You're going for the ultra-hot, bright colors and whites in the same load! If you're worried that there isn't enough color to stain the whites, grab some red food coloring from the cupboard and squirt a good amount directly onto the snowy white fabric. It's the equivalent of yellow snow on your front porch right in front of your door...it will get some serious attention.

But color transfer to whites is not the only course of action. What about darks? In a subsequent load of darks, a wonderful technique is to add bleach! It will leave its mark for sure. You'll certainly be challenged about what the heck happened. A great male response is our typical, "I dunno." If pressed, mention, "I can't ever remember what you add bleach to, but I know it's important in the cleaning process, so I took a guess. When in these situations, I just think, 'What would my mom do?'"

If you're discovering a lack of things to discolor then search her closet and drawers for tags that say, "Dry clean only," and "Hang dry only." Leather and suede items are eligible too! Let her know you didn't have a "full to the top load" so you went searching for extra things to add to the wash.

Drying With Purpose
Things that should not be dried in a dryer include leather, faux leather, latex, waterproof fabrics, rubber items, silk, wool, suede, nylon tights, and fur. Therefore, these are items that you absolutely must dry at the highest temperatures that the dryer allows. If your dryer has a setting for "Surface of the Sun" then that's the one you want! Hint: Polyester can melt at high temperatures.

The goal is shrinkage! High temperatures on certain types of clothing material can shrink them faster than that shrinkage of a politician's promises.

The very last load of clothing to be dried should be the heavy-duty things like jeans, which retain moisture well. When "drying" this last load, you should just place them into a hot dryer and close the door. Do not dry them! The warmth will help grow the mildew quickly and if you can hide them in there overnight, they will be very musty smelling upon discovery. What a memorable surprise, right?

If your wife says to be sure to hang the delicates to dry, that's a sign that you must "forget." Maybe grab some of your tidy whities and hang them to show you tried to listen but forgot what a delicate was and since these go against your manly parts, you figured they were delicate. Note, if you happen to have an old pair still kicking around since high school, especially if they have skid marks, those should be hung front and center in plain view!

Take a photo to show your buddies next time you get away. This legendary mental image in her brain will certainly be shared in her future counseling sessions and, if you play your cards right, her future thoughts of having you help with laundry will be quickly followed by a brief gag reflex as the thought of that image passes by.

If you think your bride is going to help you fold the laundry, then static electricity is your friend! Dry on the highest temperature for longest time allowed and never use a static cling thingy - those are for sissies. Synthetic fabrics like nylon and polyester are the best static generators. Even if your wife isn't helping fold these loads of laundry, these can retain a lot of voltage if you leave them mostly balled up. It's almost as electrifying as peeing on an electric fence!

If she asks you if you remembered to put a static cling sheet in the dryer, respond, "The dryer? Dang. My mom bought me a box of those in college and I could never remember whether they went in the washer or the dryer. I put them in the washer. Dang, I can never remember how to use those things!"

Folding Clothes to Keep Wrinkles In

Pack clothes directly from the dryer into a basket for a couple hours before folding. Yes, pack them! Step on them in the basket if you need to, but ensure those wrinkles are firm! For very bulky items, and assuming you're home alone, feel free to wad them into a ball and back over them with your truck to help create flat, wrinkled perfection.

When folding clothes, make a game of it and attempt to fold no two items alike. Mismatch socks that look similar, but don't be too obvious by mismatching socks that don't look anything like each other. Purposeful sock mismatching is an art that, if done right, can demonstrate believable incompetence. Never fold along seams.

Wash, Rinse, Repeat

It is important to understand that your gal will be angry, and this might be an understatement. However, try hard to look astonished and confused while she is yelling. If it gets too harsh to handle, blame your mother for not teaching you…your wife will secretly love this putdown of your mother, which can help her calm down…maybe.

Your wife may now attempt to "teach you." This is a great opportunity to practice nodding while staring blankly and quietly reciting in your mind the defensive starting line of your favorite football team.

Repeatedly offer to try again. If she ever allows you to do it again, be sure to leave a ball point pen in your least-favorite white shirt pocket before washing. Also, attempt to leave the arm of her favorite knitted sweater hanging out the drier door during drying to ensure one arm shrinks and one stretches like the 1970's toy, Stretch Armstrong.

Yes, it will ruin clothing, but the cost of a few outfits and some healthy screaming is worth the price to pay for never doing laundry again. Besides, you'll go out of your way to go shopping with her to help pick out new clothes! #EarnBackAFewBrowniePoints

You will certainly be the butt of jokes during girls' night out, but it's truly a small price to pay for a lifetime of never being asked to do the laundry again. Extremely important: Never, EVER, let this secret escape into the public domain. This is highly confidential information for men only.

When all else fails, act indignant and firmly say, "Well, that's how my mother did it!" Then quickly duck while protecting your crotch from a swift kick!

Disclaimer

It probably goes unsaid that choosing to never do laundry again will cause your lady to have some dissatisfaction with your relationship. Real men understand this and if they choose to go this route, they must make up for it in other ways. Relationships are give and take and by tricking your partner into doing the laundry all the time, you are risking an imbalance in your relationship. It's important to figure out how to offset the imbalance. Always handling folding the clothes (which can be done in front of the TV!), taking complete care of your vehicles, handling all the yard work, fixing whatever gets damaged, giving lots of backrubs, or whatever it takes – these are important decisions and many a man has ended up in divorce when he forgets that relationships need balance.

Cooking for Freedom

"In our kitchen, the recipe for disaster includes men as the main ingredient." – Anonymous

"I'm such a good cook that the fire alarm cheers me on." – Wise Man (requested anonymity)

This teaches other men how to enjoy a lifetime of never being asked to cook full meals in the kitchen.

Some men love to cook, and while that's good for marital joy, it does put pressure on the majority of men that loathe cooking. If you do enjoy cooking, you're better than most men so congratulations. However, you must understand that you should never disclose it in front of other married women, as it will cause undue stress on their husbands later when they constantly get compared to you. Take one for the team and downplay it! You can skip this chapter since you're a dude who will be a slave to the kitchen the rest of your life and you're good with that.

If you are a skilled cook and enjoy cooking (not counting at a BBQ grill), but don't want to get stuck in the home kitchen the rest of your marriage, it is essential that you, right now, make the decision to give it up [at home] to have freedom in many other ways. We'll pause here so you can dig deep and decide how much you appreciate being a man vs being a controlled wuss. If you continue to read, the assumption is to accept the fact that you will never reveal that you enjoy cooking on behalf of the other men in your community.

Prepare the Groundwork
It is important that you prepare the groundwork of this incredible feat immediately after your honeymoon. Trying to pull this off after several years of marriage is far too late and can only be accomplished slowly and

methodically by the very few social experts among us. No, you are probably not one of those legends, so if your honeymoon is a distant memory and you find yourself begrudgingly cooking instead of sitting on the couch watching ESPN, just accept the fact that you're a wussy and your job now is to try to keep a younger man from falling into the same sad destiny that has been bestowed on your life.

Caution: Do *not* attempt this during your honeymoon, the most important vacation of your marriage. The ramifications of her sudden realization of her true destiny might cause negative imprinting, resulting in serious stress in the bedroom. "Stress" might be an understatement. It's more like being transported to Siberia during a blizzard while wearing only wet boxers. Got the idea?

It will take her anywhere from a few hours to a few days, or possibly (in rare cases) forever, to get over the realization that she can't show you off to her friends as a fully trained and housebroken husband. This will hit her hard and it will invoke stress, embarrassment, and possibly anger, but it will be worth the pain. Hang in there! Us fellow men are giving you virtual shoulder punches as encouragement.

This is all about the classic bait and switch technique, which dating couples know well. Lure them in with dreams of marrying a perfect man who is fully controllable (every woman dreams of being married to a submissive robot) and then dash their "hopes of power" on the rocks once they can't get out of the contract.

If you handled your courtship well, you would have already stepped in to make a few very simple meals by now. These would only include the classic boxed mac and cheese, a tasty side dish (heavily buttered and lightly salted vegetables), and possibly a store-bought roasted chicken. Of course, you must never reveal that you *bought* the already-roasted chicken from a store until after the "gotcha cooking event" below…but you *must* reveal it at the right time. Like a good football blitz, timing is everything! The idea up to this point is that she needs to think you are at least an okay cook that can be trained to get better.

Before you pull off the big event below, if you find yourself "helping" her cook in the kitchen, be sure to play dumb and ask a lot of questions and, no matter what, do not learn too fast and be sure to repeat the same mistakes. She should start to wonder if you're cut out for meal preparation, and she will certainly talk to her friends to help create a diabolical training program to get you up to speed. These are all warning signs that you need to hurry up and put your meal-to-end-all-meals into play soon.

When you're ready to go for it, start making a big deal about telling her you want to cook her a wonderful meal all by yourself. Maybe write a note inside a nice card and present it to her or hold her hand while you tell her. Explain that you don't want her to help, not even with the shopping, and to let you plan, cook, and serve the entire thing. It will be super romantic in her mind and we suggest taking advantage of that moment and turn it into a lucky moment (wink, wink)...since...well...it might be a lot harder after the actual meal occurs.

Take time shopping for quality ingredients. It's highly recommended that you shop at Trader Joes and be sure to buy a TJ reusable bag and "accidently" leave it laying around in the kitchen. TJs turn women on for some reason so take full advantage of it. It's worth extra brownie points...you'll need lots of brownie points after tonight. If there's no TJs in your neck of the woods, figure out what trendy grocery store she loves to shop at and go there. If you have to call her to ask whether there's a taste difference between the big avocados or small avocados for the salad, that's bonus points for you. And if you buy them as hard and un-ripe as possible, that's another plus to show your ignorance.

It's very important to understand that, before the meal is served, she'll be pretty turned on by the thought of you cooking and her curiosity will want to come hang out with you in the kitchen and try to taste your creations as you're cooking. This will ruin everything so DO NOT LET HER in the kitchen. Keep re-directing her back onto a couch with a drink, a magazine, and soft music playing. Playfully insist that she must let you do all the work and that she not taste anything until it's ready. No, you don't want her to watch you [purposefully ruin this meal] so you want her to relax because you love her so much and she deserves the break while you work.

Manstakes for the Most Memorable Meal

So, let's plan out the meal that will go down into the record books. It all starts with the presentation. You must really go all out on this event.

The key to making the "meal to end all meals" is the taste, not necessarily the look. Therefore, let's lay out a gourmet spaghetti meal. It's hard to ruin spaghetti with salad and cake for dessert, right? That's exactly what she thinks. Oh, but she underestimates the creativity of a motivated man!

When you prepare this basic meal, you must make it look reasonably good. Make typical, yet purposeful, man mistakes ("manstakes") like cutting the bread in slight, but obviously varied, thicknesses and serving with a frozen stick of butter, explained later. Setting the table can certainly be full of manstakes too!

Women HATE a messy kitchen when someone else made the mess. Well, now's your chance to let your imagination run wild in ways that make Hurricane Katrina look like a breezy afternoon.

Setting the Table

Before serving the "food from hell," you must decorate the table with a great attempt. By all means, do not set the table in any manner that reflects proper etiquette.

Roll the fork in a rumpled napkin and place it in the upper right corner at an odd angle to the plate. Place the knife on the left with the blade facing outward. The spoon goes on the left side and glasses to the top left. Place a single serving spoon in the salad and another serving spoon in the spaghetti. On her water glass, be sure to wipe a little dressing around the side of the glass as if you placed it there with dirty fingers.

It Takes Meat Balls
The meatballs need to be played right. First, you must mix a binder into the meat to help hold it together during the cooking process. Raw egg and a little bit of breadcrumbs work perfectly.

If you can get away with it, without being seen, mix quite a bit of ginger into the meat as well. It won't have a strong odor but will have a very strong taste that is very un-meatball like!

The goal is to significantly undercook them. Placing the meatballs on aluminum foil and then freezing them will help ensure they stay raw and don't cook on the inside using the technique below. But you'll have to do this part many hours ahead of time so plan accordingly.

To undercook them, you have to cook the outside quickly before the heat gets deep into the ball of meat. To do this, you must turn the heat on high up under the frying pan. Make sure the frying pan is freakin' hot, then place those meatballs on the oiled pan and quickly sear the outside, turning them so the outside becomes dark brown, almost burnt. But don't leave them on the heat any longer than it takes to brown the outside.

This will ensure that while they look great on the outside, they are a vampire's delight on the inside! When she bites into them, it might be best for you to not watch too closely so you don't break out in laughter or cringe as she takes her first bite! The legendary "Stanley D. from Redmond, Washington" helped boost this result by using a syringe to inject red food coloring gel into the middle of each meatball. Edward Cullen (Twilight) would be proud!

The Limp Spaghetti Conundrum
Before you cook the spaghetti, it's essential that you first add a quarter cup of salt to the spaghetti water so when you drop in the spaghetti strands, the

noodles will absorb that sodium and taste like a horse's salt lick when she eats them. Because you might have to eat a bite too during the meal, you should probably try some ahead of time to help train your gag reflex, so it isn't surprised during the meal.

Cook the spaghetti until it starts to mush, and the strands just start to become hard to identify individually.

Sassy Sauce
Most women won't expect men to create a spaghetti sauce from scratch so it's your choice. You can go the easy route and buy a jar of sauce to be doctored up or you can create your own sauce. To keep things easy, we'll only cover using a jar of sauce below. But if you want to make your own, start with tomato paste and add similar items as those discussed below.

For real men who know that buying a jar of sauce is easier, it doesn't really matter what brand it is because...well...it won't be recognizable anyway. Empty contents into saucepan. Normally you can serve it at room temperature for a "temperature surprise" but we need to dissolve a few things and this will require heat.

First, add an eighth cup of salt and the same amount of sugar! Sweet and salty is a thing, but we're going to ensure it influences the gag reflex. You gotta heat up the sauce to get these granules to dissolve, stirring frequently. After it has all dissolved into the spaghetti sauce, you'll want to let it cool as much as possible because cold (or at least room temperature) sauce on spaghetti helps bring out...well...the "special" flavors!

Before serving, wedge cut a fresh tomato or two and mix them into the cool spaghetti sauce! Ahhh yes, just as any Italian chef would do, right? Oh, and don't forget that very special ingredient to ensure the tomatoes stay fresh, lemon juice! Add plenty of lemon juice to ensure the sauce is sweet, salty, and sour! A memorable taste to help invoke paranoia anytime she sees spaghetti over the next six months.

Crunchy Salad

When making a salad, it's important to include a lot of bitter leaves (try dandelions from your front yard – they're edible). Toss in her favorite salad dressing but before doing this, mix a quarter teaspoon of sand into the dressing. This will keep the sand from falling to the bottom or being too visible.

When "washing leaves" comes up in eventual conversation that will definitely occur AFTER she takes a crunchy bite, say that you thought you did wash them thoroughly. Mention that you're pretty sure you washed them thoroughly because it took a long time for you to get all that *dish* soap rinsed out of the leaves when you cleaned them. Practice this statement in a mirror because you gotta learn to keep a straight face for this, bruh!

Bring Home the Bread

Without being noticed, remove the butter from the freezer shortly before serving the bread. It should be firm enough to shred your bread all over the plate and you must actually do this shredding, so she sees it happening and thinks that you think it's normal.

She'll think the varied-thickness bread looks "cute" and the smells of the meatballs and spaghetti will stir her juices. Beware, however, because the taste might encourage those juices to come up and out of her mouth quickly, much like she'd respond with a mouth full of sour milk.

Although projectile vomiting is gross, it's a sure sign that the meal was a success and, most importantly, the mental imprint of your cooking will invoke similar PTSD in the future.

Having Your Cake and Not Eating It Too

The finishing touch on the menu is the dessert. Cake is always best because what you do on the inside can be covered in a tasty layer of canned icing. When you mix the batter, sneak in an eighth cup of Worcestershire Sauce. Worcestershire (properly pronounced, "WUSS-tər-shər") is an old English word meaning, "ruins cakes."

When you place the cake pan in the oven, place a wrench on the oven rack, under one side of the pan so the cake bakes at an angle steep enough to remind your new wife of the Leaning Tower of Pisa.

Add 100 degrees to whatever temperature is called for in the baking instructions. 350 degrees turns into 450 degrees. During baking, you must be attentive and set your timer! Yep, set it for 5 minutes and keep resetting it for 5 minutes. Every time the alarm goes off, you must open the oven door and then slam it closed. With all this motion, the cake should "fall" (de-puff). With the extra heat and collapsed middle, you will have created what experienced bakers affectionately call, "cake jerky."

You want it to look appetizing, although lopsided. She'll think the lopsided look is cute and it will truly excite her thinking that you are clay that she will get to mold over time. Oh boy, how she underestimates you!

Do a great job icing the cake with store-bought frosting, unaltered. You want each bite…well…the one and only bite to start out nice and sweet before the cake flavor strikes a light saber to her palette.

The Closing Act

The key to a successful "dinner to end all dinners" is to keep a straight, loving face and talk softly and sincerely with your bride throughout the meal. She will be so excited to sit down to your romantic dinner that she might not notice her first few bites. It's critically important that you are willing to eat along with her, but you must smile and be willing to swallow the meal as long as she keeps eating. If she complains about the meal, be sure to mention that you realize it's not nearly as good as her cooking. The more bites of food she eats, the better the final result will be as the nausea will exponentiate and imprint a memory of your cooking ability.

Remember, stick to the line that either you "followed the recipe" or you "made it the way your mother always made it." She'll love that last part! If she tries to tell you how you should have done it, you should stare blankly through her eyes and display the dumbest look on your face that you can muster up. Seriously, you should practice this in a mirror because you can't crack. Remember, this will set up the rest of your life like a real man!

While staring blankly, repeatedly nod your head and say, "Okay." If she's not catching that you aren't paying attention, you might have to resort to gentle arguing with her with comments like, "I disagree because I distinctly remember how my mother did it and it was nothing like you're describing," or "I don't mind cooking for you, but I don't want any help because it makes me feel hen-pecked." "What? Too much salt in the spaghetti water? Salt completely dissolves and mom never measured so neither will I."

If she brings up the wonderful cooking you did when you were dating, you get to drop the bomb that you bought everything pre-made because you wanted to impress her. These conversations should erase all glimmers of hope in her mind about you being a good option for helping her cook meals.

Throughout this whole ordeal, you MUST remain as loving as possible so the only real disaster this evening was your cooking, not you. You love her so much. You're embarrassed that it turned out so bad. You tried your best. She's a much better cook than you.

Guess what buddy? You're about to become a free man when it comes to meals! Tonight might be rather rough and it might flow into next week or even next month. You can handle celibacy for a little while. But trust that once she settles down, you won't regret it after that! Yes, you're welcome!

There is one slight problem and that pertains to your barbeque. In a later segment, we'll discuss techniques to ensure you remain the BBQ master of the house.

Avoid Getting Sucked Back into the Kitchen
Any good woman will not give up on trying to change you. She will certainly have talked with her friends within a day or two after "the dinner from hell" and how her husband (you) is very manly but horrible in the kitchen. She'll then hear from a small subset of her friends who whimsically talk about how their husband loves cooking and frequently helps in the kitchen. Yeah, those dudes are an embarrassment to our gender and cause problems for the rest of us.

Remember that those husbands are castrated sheep, and your wife will feel like a failure because her husband (you) isn't a wuss. She'll long for a wuss so she can be the center of everyone's envy at these get togethers.

When she returns, she will try to lure you back into the kitchen! She might even use intimacy as bait so be aware.

Here's how to avoid becoming controlled…

Hopefully she doesn't try to bring you back in during the NCAA tournament but if she does, it's important that you break away and go back in with love in your eyes and willingness to help. However, you need to quickly ensure that you are incompatible in the kitchen because your "help" only causes her a lot more work.

The bottom line: Make it MUCH harder for her to have you in the kitchen rather than to just let you go back and watch TV, the win-win you'll both eventually want!

She'll ask you to help with some simple tasks, usually of the "Can you get [something] for me?" When she asks, you should happily "attempt" to comply. But never be successful! She wants a teaspoon of salt, do NOT go get it directly. Go look in the refrigerator. Grab a regular teaspoon and when she corrects you, ask where the measuring spoons are and give her a tablespoon instead. Offer to add the salt yourself and be sure to add enough to draw attention when it's eaten. Make sure she distrusts whatever you do. Always take longer than if she just did it herself.

If she asks you to follow the directions for mixing the cake mix while she works on the roast, be sure to use the wrong ingredients as best you can, ensure eggshells are left in the mix, and always undermix it. She wants you to set the oven to 350 degrees, set the clock to 3:50pm. Once it's cooking, help out by boosting it to 450 degrees so it "cooks faster." Heck, that's being helpful!

When all else fails, you can "be a man" and lovingly tell her how to cook by using that incredible technique called, "mansplaining." She'll hate this so be careful. But tell her things like she's not stirring it enough, or the lettuce smells funny, or you think the heat should be higher so it cooks faster. Don't ever criticize the taste or the final result, just the process. She will not like that you're giving her advice and...well...that's the idea.

The ultimate statement is the nuclear, "My mom would have never done it that way." But be very careful because romance won't be happening in your bed for a while. This will ensure that you won't be wanted in the kitchen in the future. And although her girlfriends might convince her to try again, you can simply repeat these same steps to produce the same result.

Reward Her for Your Freedom
Good relationships are balanced. Yes, you succeeded at staying out of the kitchen. But she ended up doing all the work. That's good for your manhood and TV time, but bad for your relationship. Therefore, you need to reward her profusely. NEVER criticize the taste of her cooking, even if you must secretly choke it down. Thank her for making such a wonderful meal. Hug her, kiss her neck, and hold her waist while you thank her. Dudes need to

show their appreciation for a good woman because if you don't, someone else might!

It's okay to offer to clean up the kitchen with her, especially if it can wait until after the game. If she tries to stick you with all the cleanup because she did all the cooking, you can easily make her regret that choice by consistently doing a horrible job. That includes ensuring that food remains on "washed" plates, never drying all the water off, and frequently placing the items into the wrong locations.

This "wrong locations" technique will guarantee that she takes over this task after she has searched the entire kitchen for her measuring spoon before finding it in the spice rack. After all, it makes sense that she usually measures spices so why not store it with the spices, eh?

But the bottom line is to go out of your way thanking her and rewarding her for her awesome kitchen skills and, most importantly, frequently brag to others about her cooking and talk down your skills to help psychologically convince her that SHE does not want you in her kitchen.

Congratulations on your newfound freedom! Now what new tasks are you going to pick up around the home to help balance your part of the relationship? Real men also give back to keep balance!

Author's note: the proven techniques above are effective at giving you freedom from the kitchen, but they are also proven to cause severe marriage strain if YOU do not find a way to compensate in carrying a fair share of the workload in other ways. Keeping the cars in tune, taking care of the yard, keeping your closet organized, etc. We love our women, but we do need to be fair to them too. Real men are fair.

Maintaining BBQ Grill Master Status

"I don't know why men like to barbecue so much. Maybe it's the only thing they can cook. Or maybe they're just closet pyromaniacs." – Cecelia Ahern

"To barbecue is a way of life rather than a desirable method of cooking." – Clement Freud

There's nothing worse than having your lady take over your barbeque grill! You might as well call you doctor and set an appointment to get castrated. This chapter isn't *about* BBQing, but it is ensuring you can keep the reins on it. In the previous chapter, we learned how to stay out of the kitchen, but in this case, we need to make her want to leave the outdoor BBQ grill alone as your sacred ground.

Here is a play-by-play strategy for ensuring she leaves your BBG grill alone and lets you handle it in the future.

The Setup
The basic plan: Get her to do it without you, ensure she fails gloriously, step in as the confident master willing to handle it in the future.

The first thing you need to do is trick her into attempting to do most of the BBQ cooking herself on a particular evening. This requires a lot of pre-planning in order to allow her to fail at the BBQ. You can totally put the nail in the coffin if it's a public BBQ event, but that's pretty harsh and requires that you ensure your male buddies know what you're doing so they don't step in to help her, which they will certainly do otherwise. You don't want that to backfire since it would be more disastrous than trying to juggle flaming marshmallows.

Let's instead focus on a private BBQ event where it's just the two of you. Before you must bow out and *let* her take over, you must set up the situation carefully.

First comes the meat. Two days before the "event," you should buy two expensive cuts of meat like Tenderloin or Kobe Sirloin. Drop them both in sand and really work it into the tissue so it's embedded. Then give them a quick rinse to remove the visible sand, knowing there is a few hidden crunchy morsels of goodness for "memorable" tasting later.

Then you need to freeze one of them. Before doing this, you must memorize the shape differences. Notice fatty areas so you can easily pick out the frozen steak later...it's important that you can pick it out later. Pull it out of the freezer a few hours before the "event" and put it into the refrigerator with the unfrozen steak.

Mention to your wife that you don't want to marinate these steaks this time because you have a hankering for the awesome flavor of high-quality meat. Talk about it several times that day so she knows you're as excited as a squirrel on a caffeine high. Talk about how you know that a good salt and pepper rub is all they need for a great taste...as long as they're cooked correctly. Yep, as long as...

Show her how you like to do the rub. You do the partially frozen steak and let her do the rub on the unfrozen steak, starting with salt since it won't feel different from any sand that might be felt in the process.

Gaslighting

That morning, you must turn off the propane or natural gas to your BBQ. You want to ensure it's impossible for her to start the BBQ. If you have a big fancy manly BBQ setup with a plumbed gas line, you can go turn off the gas line feeding the BBQ. This will ensure that when she tries to light it, it won't work for her.

When you come to the rescue, ask her to get something for you in the house and while she's gone, quickly turn back on the gas and then light it with no problem. Tell her that it can be finicky sometimes, but it worked for you and you're not sure why it didn't work for her.

Mention that it's lucky there wasn't a strong gas smell because you've seen these puppies explode upon lighting if the gas is left on too long before ignition. This whole ordeal will make her leery of the BBQ itself and think she must have done something wrong.

Get Her Cooking
Here is the most important part. It requires some dramatic elements. You need a good excuse for not cooking the meat yourself. Either have a buddy call you with a fake emergency that requires a long phone conversation and your full attention so you can get her to do it for you, or you will have a sudden back spasm so you can't stand up very long, or you burnt your dominant hand really bad and need to ice it (for a miraculous healing later) or some other injury.

However, many guys decide it works best by suddenly challenging her to cook the meat and offering to give her a non-sexual backrub later as a reward...because you can guarantee that after this full event plays out, you ain't getting' no romance anyway tonight! Besides, backrubs are often irresistible to our ladies.

The Final Lap
While steaks are cooking, set the table with a few candles and turn out the rest of the lights and get some romantic music playing. You do not want her to get a good view of her steak later so keep it rather dark and romantic.

Back to the meal... as the cooking progresses, she'll need to perform the "slice and check" to see how pink it is on the inside. It is critical that you are there for this because you MUST have her cut the unfrozen steak only. Mention that you'll take that damaged piece so she can have the pristine one. What a thoughtful guy!

When she finishes cooking the steaks, offer to plate them and ensure she gets the previously frozen one, which should be as bloody as a vampire's dream.

While seated at your candlelight dinner, when she bites into it, you need to do the same to yours. Bite down carefully because the sand will not be comfortable. Watch her closely and noticeably pause while chewing. She will bite the sand and the nearly raw meat. As you look at each other, act as though you are trying not to be rude but be clear that you are not enjoying the experience of what's in your mouth. Ask her if she rotated the meat around on the grill (as if that would have cooked everything better).

Then, before she decides to put the meat back on the grill or cook a replacement meal, grab both plates, go over to the trash and dump them both. Then tell her that she doesn't need to apologize for anything and that you're taking her out to a romantic dinner. Take her hand and lead her out to the car.

You saved the evening in a romantic way, and she won't try to use your BBQ ever again!

The Barb was Queued Up
It is truly important to understand that the above scenario is not really a win-win scenario without further thought. She lost in every way when it comes to barbequing because even if you handle the grill from now on, she's often the one setting the table, preparing the side dishes, and often getting meat ready to grill, and cleaning up the dishes after...while you basically stood there with a beer, waiting for the meat to cook. And of course, you get the praise for the whole meal by guests even though what you actually did was minimal.

If you want your marriage to last, you can't let this remain too one-sided. You need to take over a few extra tasks in return and sincerely compliment and thank her for everything that she's doing. Barbequing can be a fun team sport where you get to rule the grill and she rules everything else while still earning points (see the next section about the points).

And above all, do not make her clean your grill! That's just not cool.

This page was intentionally left blank.

The Secret Point System Game That Women Play

"Behind every great man is a woman who's secretly tallying up the embarrassing things she's gotten him to do. It's all part of the master plan." – Stephen the Spy (code name)

The following information is Top Secret. It was obtained by a gay friend who was able to convince a well-liquored ladies Bunco group that he was an ally. He has shared this at tremendous risk to himself and he will forever be remembered via the code name, *Stephen the Spy*.

The Deets

Okay, here's the deets: She is playing a fiercely competitive game with her female friends. Yes, we've all suspected it and with Stephen's inside scoop, we're exposing as much of the game as we understand it. However, we know this information is incomplete, so teams around the world have attempted to piece together the facts.

In your marriage, you are stuck in a game that you can't get out of. It is basically a series of "husband embarrassing challenges." And the worst part? We never even get to see the scorecard! Some say that many have a secret app on their smartphones to keep score. Stephen said he saw a few women start with their Messenger app and do some special key sequence and it jumped into a scoring spreadsheet that looked like it had worldwide teams and various scoring and bonuses.

It's a point system and the more she can deflower your manhood, the more points she gets. She and her girlfriends are trying to get you and the rest of us men to fall for various tricks; it's truly insane. And do you know what? You'll likely fall for it!

The Score is Against You

Thanks to Stephen's insider information, we have been able to connect with other insiders and do some undercover work to figure out some of the scoring system they use! Here are the parts we have been able to put together so far. The game is played on a scoring system and while we do know that there are points awarded every time she can get you to do something that lessens your control of the relationship, we're not certain what the exact points are because they seem to be on a strange rotating basis so that what is worth a hundred points this week is only worth ten points next week. This could be why there seems to be a larger-than-normal number of couples walking in a clothing store on a given night out to dinner. It has something to do with the tasks that are bringing the most points that week.

The items below do not show the actual points, but we are certain that the bonus multipliers are fairly accurate.

Marbled Sunscreen

Points: She gets points if you let her talk you into applying sunscreen to her back at the beach. (NOTE: This item alone is worth giving her the points)

Bonus Points: If she gets you to apply it on her arms, legs, or face since she can reach those areas herself. The unfortunate thing is that it's a lot of fun and many men don't mind giving up a few points here and there, but let's face it, the score is against you and her smile is just as much about racking up the points as it is getting sunscreen lathered on.

Double Bonus Points: If you let *her* apply some to *your* back because she will purposefully never cover all your back and at the end of the day, your back will look like a marble map of burnt and non-burnt areas.

Triple Bonus Points: If she can get you to walk back to the car without a shirt on, showing off your marbled back to all the ladies who will give her a smile knowing she tripled out on you today!

Phone Call at Work

Points: She gets points if you accept a call from her while you're at work. You know it can wait and she knows it can wait and that's the whole reason she's calling you. It's for the points!

Bonus Points: For placing someone on hold in order to take the call. This shows that she's your priority and while that's a good thing in your relationship, she hears "cha-ching" in the point tally.

Double Bonus Points: If she can get you to walk out of a meeting to talk to her. Oh, this is the ultimate scoring move in this category. To get you to lightly risk your job by walking out of a meeting at work is not only brave, but it earns her points as she proves to those at your work, how much you love her.

Triple Bonus Points: If she can, in front of your coworkers, remind you to do an errand for her. These typically include shopping errands (see section later), chores at home such as vacuuming, dusting, cleaning bathrooms, etc. It's not that you don't help out around the house, but it's to declare to your coworkers who runs the show in your relationship. This public statement is definitely a triple-point move!

Hold Her Purse

Points: Hold her purse, even for a few seconds. This includes falling for the "Honey could you grab my hair clip out of my purse?" Holding a purse shouldn't be a big deal, but because they've made it point worthy, it has become equivalent to you attempting to breastfeed a child...it's just wrong and unmanly. And retrieving something from a woman's purse is not only unmanly, but it's very dangerous. Robert J. from Miami, Florida literally lost his forearm during the pandemic when something bit it off from deep inside a purse!

Bonus Points: If other women see you do it. Beware, they often sneak photos and post them on private girls-only social media groups.

Double Points: Awarded if other men see you do it. This is awarded double because it helps their cause by showing other men that they are not the only controlled dudes in relationships.

Triple Points: If she can get you to hold it in a store while she disappears, forcing you to start walking through the store, carrying the purse, looking for her. Oh, this is Nirvana for ladies and if you watch carefully, you'll notice ladies you don't even know start to follow you around the store, timing you on their watches and taking video of you to post in their secret groups.

Quadruple Points: If, while holding it, you call out her name while looking for her. Dude, we're not sure what to say here but we are lowering our heads and shaking them slowly from side to side in disappointment.

Wearing Girlyman Clothes

Points: She racks up points when she can get you to wear cheesy clothes – things you'd NEVER wear on your own.

Bonus Points: When you wear them out in public or she can post photos of you wearing them. This is the point. "See what I can get my man to do?" (replace "man" with "girlyman" in the previous sentence).

Double Points: When even a gay star from "Queer Eye for the Straight Guy" looks at you with disappointment, she wins. Let's face it, our gay brothers often have a better idea of proper fashion and if we can't impress these dudes with what she puts on us, it's a social fail all the way around.

Triple Points: If you're wearing something that matches her dog's outfit or something her ex-boyfriend wore. Seriously, it's time to drop the clothes and streak back to a testosterone safety zone.

Shopping Cart Humiliation

Points: She wins points if she can get you to push a shopping cart for her while she shops. Sounds like a gentlemanly thing to do, right? Nope, it's a trick!

Bonus Points: If you're in Trader Joes, Nugget, or a Piggly Wiggly. These boutique grocery stores are classic for finding men stuck in the shopping cart humiliation game.

Double Points: If you follow her around the store like a child wanting a binky. It will look completely random, but she is watching you out of the corner of her eye and the moment you turn your head to try to decipher a sale for rutabagas, she will dart further away and start talking to you so you can hear her voice but not understand her words. This causes you to scramble to her side, with the cart, to find out what you missed.

Extra Bonus: For every in-aisle U-Turn she can make you do while pushing the cart. Yup, your nose ring is getting tugged.

Double Points: If there is a child in the seat of the shopping cart. Mommy is merely making sure the children know who wears the pants in the family and her points double because of that.

Triple Points: If there is a box of tampons in the cart! You might as well be carrying a sign that reads, "Move over for the Wuss Express coming down the aisle!"

Quadruple Points: If her purse is in the shopping cart. Oh, it might start off on her shoulder, but it WILL end up in the cart if you're not vigilant.

Quadruple Points: If she can abandon you (ditch you) and force you to go all over the store looking for her! It's amazing how quickly they do this and end up on an aisle you previously walked down! We have multiple eye-witnesses that have seen women go hide in the restroom for a few minutes.

Automatic Monthly Win: if she gets you to have the manager make an announcement over the loudspeakers looking for your lost wife! Buddy, you're toast...milk toast!

Run to the Store for "A Few Things"

Points: "Oh honey, here, I made you a list." You know your wife's a genius when she can turn a simple grocery run into an epic adventure in husband humiliation.

Extra Bonus: Unusual spices, vegetable bouillon cubes, or a very specific brand of food coloring. You can be certain she already knows that the store you are going to doesn't carry the product and there will always...ALWAYS be one of these items on the shopping list. These are bonus items that give her points if you call or text her to ask where they are located in the store. She gets double bonus points if you attempt to go to another store to find them. If you actually want to find the item, you should probably just go to Trader Joe's to start with (or whatever similar boutique grocery store she usually shops at) since it's her little joke to list these items on your shopping list for a conventional store that doesn't carry them.

Double Points: Vague items such as "Can of beans." It doesn't matter what kind of beans you are thinking about because you'll be wrong! Green beans? Black beans? Kidney, pinto, white, chili, lima, refried, or garbanzo beans? It won't matter because it will never be what you're thinking. She gets a major bonus for getting you to go back to the store, so your only strategy to beat this game is to buy one of every single type of canned bean in the store. Yes, it will be a LOT, but she will *never* try that trick on you again! Although you better be ready to go back to the store to return all the cans that she didn't want...and yes, she gets a bonus for that too!

Triple Points: The dreaded, epic, "Tampons" shopping list item. Just getting you to go to the store with that item on the list is worth double points! The known embarrassment at the checkout counter is her thrill, so if tampons are the only thing on the list, you must ensure there are other things in the cart to counteract it (to dilute the embarrassment). Real men put it on the counter along with a protein shake and box of condoms, making the cashier confused and blushed at the thought of you "running the red light."

But how do you handle the purchase to minimize her points? Well, the trick is returning home with tampons that are completely unusable OR one of everything. If your bride is a larger woman, you need to find the smallest size available. Even if you must ask for help, be sure to ask for tampons that would fit a "young teenage daughter who is very petite and skinny." Remember the phrase, "Buy petite and save the receipt." If your bride is slim and petite, you go for the extra-large size which we assume contains something resembling a roll of paper towels with attached yachting rope.

Of course, men have no clue what is inside that tampon box because we don't want to know out of fear of it ruining our sex drive for eternity. But make sure that whatever you bring back isn't what she might expect. If she seems offended, just explain that you are extremely uncomfortable on that aisle, so you did a quick drive-by, quickly grabbing what you thought seemed reasonable. If you ended up grabbing one of everything, it will be ultra-annoying, especially if you refuse to return them because she'll get stuck with it and certainly won't want to do it again.

Rolling with the Punches
The unfortunate reality is that many women play these games. Real men work to minimize their total points. But unless your woman is in a coma, they *will* control you and they *will* gain some points every day. It's inevitable if you want to be in a relationship. Your goal is to figure out what you're willing to purposefully give up. Your relationship is going to be pretty lame if you refuse to let your gal gain any points at all. Heck, you might as well be single and celibate.

It takes a real man to understand that being in love requires small sacrifices and "letting" her have some points. She will not enjoy being in a relationship with you unless you play along a little bit. It does have its rewards, so either way you need to figure out how to cash in on those rewards.

IMPORTANT: If you appreciate the humor in this book and would like to give back or thank the author, PLEASE leave a review at Amazon and/or other major book resellers as positive reviews boost rankings. If you didn't enjoy this book...well...ummm...hey, no need to waste your time. 😊

www.ingramcontent.com/pod-product-compliance
Lightning Source LLC
Chambersburg PA
CBHW070041080526
44586CB00013B/876